ragamuffin books

If you are enjoying this notebook, please consider leaving a review. We would appreciate it very much.

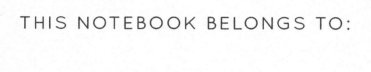

THIS NOTEBOOK BELONGS TO:

Made in United States
Orlando, FL
16 December 2023

40992883R00064